MOVING IN HIS MAJESTY & POWER

MOVING IN HIS MAJESTY & POWER

NEAL A. MAXWELL

DESERET
BOOK

SALT LAKE CITY, UTAH

Library of Congress Cataloging-in-Publication Data

Maxwell, Neal A.
  Moving in His majesty and power / Neal A. Maxwell.
      p. cm.
  Includes bibliographical references and index.
  ISBN 1-59038-393-1 (hardbound : alk. paper)
  1. Christian life—Mormon authors. 2. Providence and government of God.
3. Church of Jesus Christ of Latter-day Saints—Doctrines. 4. Mormon
Church—Doctrines. I. Title.
  BX8656.M366 2004
  248.4'89332—dc22
                                          2004017445

Printed in the United States of America   72076
Publishers Printing, Salt Lake City, Utah

10   9   8   7   6   5   4   3   2   1

To my precious wife,
family, and friends, and
to faithful disciples everywhere

Little people like you and me, if our prayers are sometimes granted, beyond all hope and probability, had better not draw hasty conclusions to our own advantage. If we were stronger, we might be less tenderly treated. If we were braver, we might be sent, with far less help, to defend far more desperate posts in the great battle.

C. S. Lewis

CONTENTS

Contents

FOREWORD

My FATHER FINISHED WORKING on the manuscript of this book just ten days before he passed away. By that time he had little energy, but in the last weeks of his life, he was focused intently on two almost-consuming priorities: spending time with his family, including giving blessings to grandchildren who had not yet received one, and finishing his last manuscript.

As these priorities exemplify, Neal A. Maxwell was a teacher. He loved the word of the Lord. He believed with the psalmist that the word of the Lord "is a lamp unto my feet, and a light unto my path" (Psalm 119:105). He observed, "When one sees life and people through the lens of His gospel, then one can see for-ever" (*Ensign*, May 1974, 112). That perspective guided his life's work.

Dad often said the gospel was inexhaustible, and his actions underscored that belief. The gospel was for him an endless source of truth and joy; he found the study of it invigorating. He taught it in his daily walk and talk and through his sermons and books. His desire to capture in words the insights and connections his perceptive mind noted stayed with him throughout his mortal life.

At my father's funeral, President Gordon B. Hinckley noted: "I know of no other who spoke in such a distinctive and interesting way. When he opened his mouth we all listened. We came alive with expectation of something unusual, and we were never disappointed. . . . Each talk was a masterpiece, each book a work of art, worthy of repeated reading. I think we shall not see one like him again" (*Church News*, 31 July 2004, 3).

Moving in His Majesty and Power is the last install-ment in Elder Maxwell's printed legacy. It includes, in revised form, three talks he gave in the last two years of his life and which he felt were worthy of publication. It also includes a section of succinct, penetrating gospel insights on a wide variety of topics, similar in format to that of his previous work, W*hom the Lord Loveth.*

I hope you will enjoy this book. More importantly, though, I hope my father's objective in writing it will be achieved, namely, to help us resolve to become more committed disciples and to deepen our gratitude for the inexhaustible gospel he loved so deeply and proclaimed so tirelessly.

CORY H. MAXWELL

Acknowledgments

I ALONE AM RESPONSIBLE for the contents of this volume, which is not an official publication of The Church of Jesus Christ of Latter-day Saints.

Especially deserving of thanks are Edward J. Brandt and Max H. Molgard, who contributed a doctrinal review with confirmation and suggestions. Susan Jackson, a remarkable secretary, displayed her patience and skill once again but in even greater abundance. Suzanne Brady of Deseret Book diligently performed the necessary editing.

As always, my son, Cory H. Maxwell, was helpful by encouraging the book's completion.

Colleen, the exceptional caregiver, encouraged this

project while ministering so thoughtfully and constantly to me as well.

FREE TO CHOOSE

THE DOCTRINE OF OUR FREEDOM to choose is not fully presented in the precious Holy Bible. Blessedly, key verses have been given to us in the breakthroughs provided by Restoration scriptures. Said Lehi: "Men are free according to the flesh; and all things are given them which are expedient unto man. And they are free to choose liberty and eternal life, through the great Mediator of all men, or to choose captivity and death, according to the captivity and power of the devil; for he seeketh that all men might be miserable like unto himself" (2 Nephi 2:27).

The vital revelations about the agency of man—our

freedom to choose—inevitably disclose the perfect generosity and justice of God. Simultaneously, they show how deeply serious God is about human joy and about the necessity of our having moral agency in order to achieve a later fullness of joy.

Likewise, these revelations disclose His sublime character. The Prophet Joseph Smith declared, "If men do not comprehend the character of God, they do not comprehend themselves" (*Teachings of the Prophet Joseph Smith,* 343). No wonder so many mortals are strangers to themselves as they twist and turn to avoid facing their true identity.

When trying to comprehend and to apply such a grand doctrine, however, we display sheer naivete at times. Though declarative regarding agency, fundamentals such as these underscore our underappreciation:

1. *"I [have given] unto man his agency"* (Moses 7:32; italics added; see also D&C 101:78; Moses 4:3; JST Genesis 3:4).

Agency is such a great gift, and yet we sometimes barely get beyond examining the outer wrappings.

2. "Thou mayest *choose for thyself*" (Moses 3:17; italics added).

The ultimately sovereign self!

Of course, our genes, circumstances, and environments matter very much, and they shape us significantly; yet, there remains an inner zone in which we are sovereign. In this zone lies the very essence of our individuality and our personal accountability.

So many spiritual outcomes require saving truths to be mixed with time, forming the elixir of experience. Desire denotes a deep inner longing or craving, more than passive preferences or fleeting feelings.

In the agonizing atoning process, Jesus let His will be "swallowed up in the will of the Father" (Mosiah 15:7). As sovereigns, we choose to yield to the Highest Sovereign as our highest act of choice. It is the only surrender which is also a victory!

3. "That ye may live and move and do *according to your own will*" (Mosiah 2:21; italics added). God will not use compulsory means. In contrast, almost all of us

are quite willing to use such means ourselves at times (see D&C 121:39).

God's granting of agency is so complete and personal. It is so breathtaking! With first realizations there is understandably initial exhilaration, but beside it a disquieting realization also emerges. Satan actually "sought to destroy the agency of man," beginning with the war so vigorously fought in the premortal world (Moses 4:3; see also Revelation 12:7). The clash between the need for our agency and Lucifer's desires for ascendancy were the causes. Everything else was ancillary in those distant, formative moments—just as everything else will finally be ancillary to the reality of the Resurrection.

4. *"Act according to [our] wills* and pleasures, *whether to do evil or to do good"* (Alma 12:31; italics added).

Why does the stern, divine candor fixing final accountability seem so repetitive?

5. "Whosoever doeth iniquity, *doeth it unto himself;* for behold, ye are free" (Helaman 14:30; italics added).

There is always at least one victim of iniquity. Yes, I am free to choose, but I can neither be immune from the consequences of my wrong choices nor avoid accountability (see Romans 14:12; D&C 101:78). Hence the accompanying disquietude. Life must be so.

Walter Bagehot perceptively observed: "A sun that shines and a rain which falls equally on the evil and on the good, are essential to morality in a being free like man" (*Works of Walter Bagehot,* 2:313). Professor Matthew Holland noted how Thomas Jefferson wrote similarly of how "some divine power he calls 'god' has 'formed us as moral agents'" ("'Circle of Our Felicities,'" 202).

Truly, our freedom to choose is a shining and shimmering gift, but it is also one that can cause some shivering at times. Is this why, so poised, we are sometimes almost afraid to decide certain things? Are we afraid we might make a mistake? Do we realize why stalling or "no decision" is a decision?

Unrepented-of mistakes bring a measure of self-hatred. Hence, at the point of decision, our emitting a soul sigh is permissible: Choosing is no casual picnic, after all, but it prepares the righteous for the later celebratory supper of the Lord (see D&C 58:9).

Furthermore, we are not left alone! Mercifully, each of us has within us the guiding light of Christ. We can actually distinguish between good and evil. Yes, accept it or not, we really are sufficiently instructed that we know good from evil (see 2 Nephi 2:5; Moroni 7:16, 19). This fact is fundamental, but do we really believe it? Especially as the human scene oozes further its spreading evils?

Most mercifully, we can repent. Further, the Holy Ghost can guide us and reassure us. His gifts include peace and joy and love—of which there is such an ongoing shortage in the world! Such is the precious and pervading sunshine of the Spirit which, if we will receive it, can pierce the darkest of moments and circumstances (see Galatians 5:22; James 1:17; Moroni 10:8, 17).

Therefore, we are not left alone! Nevertheless, we are clearly and constantly at risk.

6. "[You will receive] according to *[your] desire*" (Alma 29:4; italics added).

7. "[And you will receive] according to *[your] wills*" (Alma 29:4; italics added).

Do we truly grasp how the final Judgment will actually reflect our choices—a different thing from having some final box score arbitrarily handed down from on high? Our on-the-record desires and cumulative choices will prevail! How manifestly just of God! How trembling for me! Are my desires sufficiently educated to choose wisely? (see Alma 13:3, 10). Could the further education of my desires thus be the most important form of my continuing education? President Joseph F. Smith taught:

"God's ways of educating our desires are, of course, always the most perfect. . . . And what is God's way? Everywhere in nature we are taught the lessons of patience and waiting. We want things a long time before we get them, and the fact that we wanted them a long time makes them all the more precious when they come. In nature we have our seedtime and harvest; and if children were taught that the desires that they sow may be reaped by and by through patience and labor, they will learn to appreciate whenever a long-looked-for goal has been reached. Nature resists us and keeps admonishing us to wait; indeed, we are compelled to wait" (*Gospel Doctrine,* 297–98).

So it is that the chilly dawn of realization is further felt: Real choosing actually bristles with alternatives, enticements, defining moments, accountability, counterfeits, and consequences!

8. Why then do some choose to remain "*willingly . . . ignorant*" of various revelations? (2 Peter 3:5; italics added). Some seem to say, "My mind is made up, so don't confuse me with cosmic facts. Instead, let me try to compartmentalize my life and my choices, and I'll do things my way."

Ripe with implications, Restoration scriptures inform us that some of the worst rebels are simply—

9. "*Not willing* to enjoy that which they might have received" (D&C 88:32; italics added).

A cold wind of reality blows steadily at the edges of

our minds. Foregoing enjoyment? But why? Knowingly turning down something vastly better? Why? So our outcome really is our choice. No one can even allege he has received a raw deal (see Mosiah 16:1; 27:31; Alma 12:15).

Thus, some know the will of God but still "wilfully rebel against God" (3 Nephi 6:18). How can such obviously self-damaging choices be made?

This is a real and ongoing war—with real casualties—in which there can be neither neutrals nor pacifists. No wonder the persistence of the wry quip, born of frustration, regarding "free agency and how to enforce it."

In effect, some, by their indifferent behavior, seem almost to ask, "Is this grand gift perhaps returnable?" Others simply do not like living in a choice-filled world with genuine accountability.

10. "For, behold, *the devil . . . rebelled against me . . .* ; and *also a third part of the hosts of heaven* turned he away from me *because of their agency*" (D&C 29:36; italics added).

Lucifer was very angry then, and he is very angry still—striving to make "all men . . . miserable like unto himself" (2 Nephi 2:27). One-third deliberately chose not to undergo the mortal experience.

It all began such a very long time ago, because—

11. "It must needs be that the devil should tempt the children of men, or they could not be *agents unto themselves*" (D&C 29:39; italics added).

12. "Wherefore, the Lord God gave unto *man* that he *should act for himself.* Wherefore, man could not act for himself save it should be that he was *enticed by the one or the other*" (2 Nephi 2:16; italics added). There really are *no* "safe" mistakes.

Furthermore, our choices are not to be made among passive, unattractive alternatives but among vibrant, alluring choices! Instead, why can't we just glide through life and cherry-pick what we want? Why must there be "an opposition in all things"? (2 Nephi 2:11). It seems so relentless at times!

13. "That *every man may act in doctrine . . . according to the moral agency which I have given unto him, that every*

man may be *accountable* for his own sins in the day of judgment" (D&C 101:78; italics added). Life being so structured, though we are not accountable for Adam's transgression, neither is God for ours! (see Article of Faith 2).

By now, any earlier exhilaration has fully departed. Instead, we see unsmiling accountability standing astride every path, hovering over every choice!

The revealed record shows that Lucifer clearly chose to seek his personal preeminence, chose to be angry when he was rejected, chose to lead others astray, and chose misery, not joy. His "one-third" followers, in turn, chose to respond to his false allures. Incredibly, they turned their collective backs on the second estate, as he remains incurably and ironically intoxicated with his desire to control others!

Nevertheless, there is a vital and reassuring ground rule: The Prophet Joseph assured us: "The devil *could not* compel mankind to do evil" and "God *would not* exert any compulsory means" (*Teachings of the Prophet*

Joseph Smith, 187; italics added). Such is our "free to choose" situation.

If we just glance at spiritual history, no wonder there is this touching lamentation from long-suffering Jesus, or Jehovah. When speaking of ancient Israel, He said, "How oft would I have gathered you as a hen gathereth her chickens, and ye would not" (3 Nephi 10:5). The "how-oft" question is one of the most haunting and reverberating in all of eternity (see also Luke 13:34).

It is matched by what the Lord of the vineyard can justifiably say at the end of the salvational day. His words make one weep. As He surveys all that He has tried to do to regenerate—while resolutely leaving us free—and given all that might have been, He, the Lord of the vineyard, tenderly asks, "What could I have done more?" (Jacob 5:47).

Oh, the special redemptive character of God, captured so eloquently by President J. Reuben Clark Jr.:

"I believe that in his justice and mercy [God] will give us the maximum reward for our acts, give us all that he can give, and in the reverse, I believe that he will impose upon us the minimum penalty which it is possible for him to impose" (Conference Report, October 1953, 84).

We read the verse about how Lucifer does not understand "the mind of God" (Moses 4:6). This failure includes Lucifer's catastrophic failure to comprehend or to accept the inviolate interplay of agency and joy.

Again, there can be no agency avoidance. *No* decision is a decision. Delay is a delusion. A delay always disdains the holy present.

Hence, choosing to be obedient is a choice. Jesus, for example, chose to let His will be "swallowed up in the will of the Father" (Mosiah 15:7). It was His deliberate choice—a choice, of course, that blessed all mortals mightily and everlastingly. Being obedient is a way *of* life, but it is also the way *to* eternal life.

Consider that scripturally intriguing phrase "compound in one," involving our freedom to choose. Without being able to choose among alternatives, we would find life to be no life at all. Things would "remain as dead," having "neither sense nor insensibility" (2 Nephi 2:11).

We are actually told that God's creation would have been wasted and would have served "no purpose," a divine declaration full of so many implications (2 Nephi 2:12). Do we comprehend that alternative and its grimness sufficiently? Sweeping words illustrating the significance of this strong doctrine, indeed!

One marvels over the extent of the cradling cosmos with its encompassing vastness and personalness. It is difficult even to contemplate adequately His cosmos and our planet's place in God's plans. In the midst of it all, God's grand gift to us is still the freedom to choose.

There are literally, science says, more stars in the universe than there are grains of sand in all the beaches, the deserts, and ocean floors on this planet (see Heinrichs, "Stellar Census"; Sagan, *Cosmos,* 196). Revealed words about numeracy are not just elegant, extravagant language. Besides, souls matter more than stars and planets!

And God wants us to have joy, which is the purpose of His creation (see 2 Nephi 2:25). We cannot do that if we "remain as dead" (2 Nephi 2:11) and unless we are free to choose to become more spiritually submissive to the God of that cosmos.

He knows how happiness is obtained. People truly matter more than stars do. Despite their longevity, we have never seen an immortal star, but, thanks to Jesus, we are immortal!

The grandness of this doctrine is beyond our comprehension, but it is not beyond receiving our added appreciative attention and exploration. We can worship with deep faith a God whose character is so stunning and who wants us to come home. But He will not force us. We must choose. He will not force us Home where, as He says, He will give us "all that he hath" (Luke 12:44). There isn't any more!

Unexplored by me until recently are the profound lessons and gospel glimpses contained in Doctrine and Covenants 29:36. Therein we read of how one-third of Heavenly Father's children were turned away from Him. This was not, so to speak, Lucifer's parliamentary rejection of God's Plan A in favor of his own Plan B.

The result was an immense, personal loss on the part of the Father. The "heavens wept over" Lucifer, His "son of the morning" (D&C 76:26), who rejected the Father and turned away from Him a third of His children "because of their agency," evoking emotion unimaginable to us on our mortal level (D&C 29:36).

Yet, in small ways, such as when our posterity turn away not only from God's plan but from us, we can sense a similar sorrow. Again, God underscores unmistakably the fact that Lucifer *rebelled against me* (Moses 4:3; italics added). Surely this rejection of the Father by a son foreshadowed so many of history's later, unresolved father-and-son differences.

This was done, too, using the very agency that God had given to Lucifer (see Moses 4:3). The irony is inescapable, the sting so sharp! Lucifer really would have destroyed our agency as part of achieving his ascendancy, all the while using the agency God had given him.

Oh, the personal rejection which permeated that awful moment. The lamentation is so laden, portraying one more reminder of what the Father has gone through.

Enoch, later, saw the God of heaven weep because of human suffering resulting from man's failure to keep His commandments to love Him and one another (see Moses 7:24, 28). When Enoch saw the heavens weep, they reflected the same drenching and wrenching feelings of the Father (see Moses 7:29, 33).

Still, even in the agony of such ultimate rejection, we see "God moving in his majesty and power" (D&C 88:47).

And all for us!

THE COSMOS

❧

THESE WORDS OF ANSELM constitute good counsel: "Believe in order to understand" (*St. Anselm,* 7), rather than understand in order to believe. If we believe in Restoration revelation, we will understand so many things.

"The scriptures are laid before thee, yea, and all things denote there is a God; yea, even the earth, and all things that are upon the face of it, yea, and its motion, yea, and also all the planets which move in their regular form do witness that there is a Supreme Creator" (Alma 30:44).

"Behold, . . . all things are created and made to bear

record of [God] . . . things which are in the heavens above, and things which are on the earth, . . . *all things bear record of me*" (Moses 6:63; italics added).

Under the Father's direction, Christ was and is the Lord of the Universe, "the same which looked upon the wide expanse of eternity" (D&C 38:1).

A few scientists share our belief in religious explanations concerning these vast creations, but others do not, some even viewing ours as an unsponsored universe and humans as beings "wrenched whimpering into an alien universe" (West, *Tower of Babel,* 183). Resoundingly, the restored scriptures tell us the cosmic facts!

But do the sweeping, scriptural words with which we have been blessed stir us enough? Are we steadily becoming the "manner of persons" who reflect such soaring doctrines by their increased spiritual sanctification? (2 Peter 3:11). God is giving away the spiritual secrets of the universe, but are we listening? In the perplexities and crunches of life, will we have sufficient faith in the Creator's having made "ample provision" to bring all His purposes to pass? (Smith, *Teachings of the Prophet Joseph Smith,* 220).

President J. Reuben Clark made this comforting comment: "Our Lord is not a novice, he is not an amateur; he has been over this course time and time and time again" (*Behold the Lamb of God,* 17). The Lord himself described His course as "one eternal round" (D&C 3:2; see also 35:1; 1 Nephi 10:19; Alma 7:20).

One scientist, who probably does not believe in divine design, nevertheless noted that "as we look out into the universe and identify the many accidents of physics and astronomy that have worked together to our benefit, it almost seems as if the universe must in some sense have known that we were coming" (Dyson, "Energy in the Universe," 59).

Whatever the "how" of God's creative process, spiritually reassuring things about the "why" are set forth about the beginning—the "back of beyond," so very long ago.

"And there stood one among them that was like unto God, and he said unto those who were with him:

We will go down, for there is space there, and we will take of these materials, and *we will make an earth whereon these may dwell.*

" . . . And they went down at the beginning, and they . . . organized and formed the heavens and the earth" (Abraham 3:24; 4:1; italics added).

Strikingly, one scientist wrote that "our galaxy, the Milky Way, is located in one of the relatively empty spaces between the Great Walls" (Strauss, "Clusters of Galaxies").

"And as one earth shall pass away, and the heavens thereof even so shall another come" (Moses 1:38).

"For behold, there are many worlds that have passed away by the word of my power" (Moses 1:35).

Of the universe and the Atonement, we sing that we "scarce can take it in"! ("How Great Thou Art," *Hymns,* no. 86).

Whatever God's initial process, there was and is apparently some intriguing divine overseeing: "And the Gods watched those things which they had ordered until they obeyed" (Abraham 4:18; italics added).

We here on this earth are not alone in the universe: "By him [Christ], and through him, and of him, the worlds are and were created, and the inhabitants thereof are begotten sons and daughters unto God" (D&C 76:24; italics added; see also Moses 1:35).

We do not know how many other inhabited planets there are or where they may be, even though we appear to be alone in our own solar system.

As to the Lord's role amid His vast other creations, so little has been revealed. There are inklings, however. Consider the parable of the lord and his servants (see D&C 88:51–60). "Therefore, unto this parable I will liken all these kingdoms, and the inhabitants thereof— every kingdom in its hour, and in its time, and in its season, even according to the decree which God hath made" (D&C 88:61).

The Lord even invites us to "ponder, in [our] hearts" that particular parable (D&C 88:62). Such pondering does not mean idle speculation but, rather, patient and meek anticipation of further revelations. Besides, God gave only partial disclosure—"not all"—

to Moses, with "only an account of this earth," but Moses still learned things he "never had supposed" (Moses 1:4, 35, 10).

We surely do not worship a one-planet God!

The vastness of the Lord's creations is matched by the personalness of His purposes. "For thus saith the Lord that created the heavens; God himself that formed the earth and made it; he hath established it, he created it not in vain, he formed it to be inhabited" (Isaiah 45:18; see also Ephesians 3:9; Hebrews 1:2).

"And worlds without number have I created; and I also created them for mine own purpose; . . . for behold, there are many worlds that have passed away by the word of my power. And there are many that now stand, and innumerable are they unto man; but all things are numbered unto me, for they are mine and I know them" (Moses 1:33, 35; italics added).

One may ask, What is God's purpose for earth's inhabitants? It is best expressed in that terse verse with which we are all so familiar: "For behold, this is my work and my glory—to bring to pass the immortality and eternal life of man" (Moses 1:39).

Therefore, in the expansiveness of space, there is stunning personalness, for God knows and loves each one of us! (see 1 Nephi 11:17). We are not meaningless ciphers floating in unexplained space. Although the psalmist's query was, "What is man, that thou art mindful of him?" (Psalm 8:4), mankind is actually at the very center of God's work. We are the "sheep of his hand" and the "people of his pasture" (Psalm 95:7; see also 79:13; 100:3). His work includes our immortalization—accomplished by Christ's glorious atonement. Think of it! Even with their extensive longevity, stars are not immortal—but we are!

The revelations give us very little information about how the Lord created it all.

Dr. Allen Sandage, a believer in divine design, was one of Edwin Hubble's two graduate students. Sandage wrote: "Science . . . is concerned with the *what, when,* and *how.* It does not, and indeed cannot, answer within its method (powerful as that method is), *why*" ("Scientist Reflects on Religious Belief," 2).

Albert Einstein said of his desires: "I want to know *how* God created this world. I am not interested in this or that phenomenon, in the spectrum of this or that element. I want to know His thoughts, the rest are details" (cited in Clark, *Einstein,* 37; italics added).

Alas, even given the remarkable revelations about the cosmos and God's purposes, people can still drift away. Astonishingly, some people have: "And it came to pass that . . . the people began to forget those signs and wonders which they had heard, and began to be less and less astonished at a sign or a wonder from heaven, insomuch that they began to be hard in their hearts, and blind in their minds, and began to disbelieve all which they had heard and seen" (3 Nephi 2:1).

As we gasp over what the Lord has created, we are to reverence Him and His character enough to strive to become ever more like Him, as He has directed (see Matthew 5:48; 3 Nephi 12:48; 27:27).

Thus, as we enlarge our views, both of the universe

and of God's stretching purposes, we, too, can reverently exclaim, "O how great the plan of our God!" (2 Nephi 9:13).

Alas, in our age, some arrogantly believe that if they cannot comprehend something, then God cannot comprehend it, either (see Mosiah 4:9).

Whatever Moses' own sample, no wonder he was overwhelmed and "fell unto the earth," saying that "man is nothing" (Moses 1:9, 10). Mercifully, the revelations assure us of God's love:

"Now my brethren, we see that God is mindful of every people, whatsoever land they may be in; yea, he numbereth his people, and his bowels of mercy are over all the earth. Now this is my joy, and my great thanksgiving; yea, and I will give thanks unto my God forever" (Alma 26:37).

Divine determination is so reassuring, as these words in Abraham set forth: "There is nothing that the Lord thy God shall take in his heart to do but what he will do it" (Abraham 3:17). His capacity is such, and, courteously but pointedly, He reminds us twice in two verses that He really is able to do His own work! (see 2 Nephi 27:20–21).

Clearly, the earth never was the center of the universe as many once provincially believed! Yet it has not been many decades since many likewise believed our Milky Way Galaxy was the only galaxy in the universe.

But the more we know, the more vital the "why?" questions and the answers thereto become. Yet the answers to the "why?" questions are obtainable only by revelations given by God the Creator, and, though these startling verses are unnoticed, much more is yet to come:

"All thrones and dominions, principalities and powers, shall be revealed and set forth upon all who have endured valiantly for the gospel of Jesus Christ.

"And also, if there be bounds set to the heavens or to the seas, or to the dry land, or to the sun, moon, or stars—

"All the times of their revolutions, all the appointed days, months, and years, and all the days of their days, months, and years, and all their glories, laws, and set times, shall be revealed in the days of the dispensation of the fulness of times" (D&C 121:29–31).

What a stunning, specific promise yet to be fulfilled!

Therefore, as we look at the universe, we do not see unexplained chaos or cosmic churn. Instead, the faithful once again see "God moving in his majesty and power" (D&C 88:47). It is like viewing a divinely choreographed, cosmic ballet—spectacular, subduing, and reassuring!

We know the Creator of the universe is also the Author of the plan of happiness. We can trust Him. He knows perfectly what brings happiness to His children, whom He loves perfectly (see Mosiah 2:41; Alma 41:10). Mercifully, His redemptive course is "one eternal round" (D&C 3:2).

"UNTO THIS VERY PURPOSE"

ILLUSTRATIVE OF THE INTERPLAY of man's agency and God's supremacy, the scriptures contain many glistening jewels over which we pass too lightly. The compressed truth in these doctrinal diamonds defies our present and full comprehension. Moreover, not only do such divine declarations come without detailed explanations but they are laden with many implications, if we are to understand God's dealings with His children (see 2 Nephi 2:12; Mosiah 10:14).

One such cluster has to do with the unique founding of this American nation, wherein the Lord revealed that He had established the Constitution of the United

States "by the hands of wise men whom [He] raised up unto this very purpose" (D&C 101:80). No parallel declaration exists with regard to the constitution of any other nation, ours being the first written constitution. Given in 1833 in Ohio, these verses were part of the Kirtland cascade of revelations. Moreover, revealed words, such as "unto this very purpose," clearly remind us that God's hand is in the details of such things— sometimes obviously, sometimes subtly.

If pondered—both as to its substance and the miraculous process of its coming forth—the Constitution is deserving of our prolonged, spiritual applause.

Think of all the Lord oversaw, including the shaping events which of necessity occurred long before the Constitution was written, ratified, and implemented. First, it was necessary for God to cause a handful of highly talented and "wise" individuals to be "raised up" (D&C 101:80). Second, they needed to live in one geographic area on this planet. Third, this contiguity also had to occur within a short time frame! Fourth, a citizenry had to be prepared who wanted and would then implement self-governance. This incubation was as important as the later ratification. Thus, the words *raised up* involve multiple and concurrent conditions. Without similar incubation, establishing modern republics and democracies has not proven easy. Founders were required but also foundational building blocks. Otherwise, holding elections could have been cathartic but not, finally, consequential.

The late historian Barbara Tuchman noted how our Founding Fathers have been called "the most remarkable generation of public men in the history of the United States or perhaps of any other nation." She observed that "it would be invaluable if we could know what produced this burst of talent from a base of only two and a half million inhabitants" (*March of Folly,* 18). Restoration revelations tell us why.

One who fought for freedom in the War for Independence was asked why he fought. Was it the Stamp Act? The Tea Party? Or reading Locke? He replied in the negative, saying, "Young man, what we meant in going for those Redcoats was this: we always had governed ourselves and we always meant to. They didn't mean we should" (cited in Fischer, *Paul Revere's Ride,* 164). Such citizen soil required much preparatory work.

President Wilford Woodruff boldly declared in general conference in April 1898:

"I am going to bear my testimony to this assembly, if I never do it again in my life, that those men who laid the foundation of this American government and signed the Declaration of Independence were the best spirits the God of heaven could find on the face of the earth. They were choice spirits, not wicked men. General Washington and all the men that labored for the purpose were inspired of the Lord" (Conference Report, April 1898, 89).

Imperfections were there, to be sure, as historian Ron Chernow reminds us: "A contradictory environment was probably an inescapable part of the transition from the lofty idealism of Revolution to the gritty realities of quotidian politics. The heroes of 1776 and 1787 were bound to seem smaller and more hypocritical as they jockeyed for personal power and advantage in the new government" (*Alexander Hamilton,* 275).

Alexander Hamilton himself wrote: "It is an observation as just as it is common that in those great revolutions which occasionally convulse society, human nature never fails to be brought forward in its brightest as well as in its blackest colors. And it has very properly been ranked not among the least of the advantages which compensate for the evils they produce that they serve to bring to light talents and virtues which might otherwise have languished in obscurity or only shot forth a few scattered and wandering rays" (cited in Chernow, *Alexander Hamilton,* 284).

Some individuals who achieve great things may soon slip into small matters (such as squabbling over the location of the capital of the United States), and smallness instead of the greatness comes to the surface.

This nation was blessed not only with Washington's wisdom and prestige but also by his superb character. One of his biographers wrote:

"In all history few men who possessed unassailable

power have used that power so gently and self-effacingly for what their best instincts told them was the welfare of their neighbors and all mankind" (Flexner, *Washington,* xvi).

Washington was the rare man who would not be king!

God raised up both the Founders and the necessary supporting cast. Involved, therefore, were the obvious luminaries—Washington, Adams, Jefferson, Hamilton, Madison, Franklin, and so forth—and also, for example, John Marshall, who was designated by his biographer Jean Edward Smith as the "definer of a nation" (*John Marshall: Definer of a Nation*).

Reflect on the foliage of the precious First Amendment. I read somewhere of the contrast between a banyan tree and a Lombardy poplar, a relevant metaphor. The latter, though a thing of beauty and symmetry, does not really offer much shade from the heat of the day or shelter from the storm, whereas a banyan tree is thick with foliage and has sturdy, wide branches. How ironic, therefore, for some to neglect to nourish certain branches of that First Amendment tree under which many would seek shelter later on. A persistent preoccupation with "freedom of speech" to the neglect of other freedoms can diminish the shelter available for religion and other precious freedoms. The intertwining of all our freedoms is greater than we realize. Citizen soil still needs continued preparation to sustain the Constitution.

Clearly, God cares about how power is handled everywhere. It is likewise clear that He also desires to protect all mortals by means of certain rights and principles:

"According to the laws and constitution of the people, which I have suffered to be established, and should be maintained for the rights and protection of all flesh, according to just and holy principles" (D&C 101:77).

The ongoing tug-of-war regarding power and the preeminence of contending values continues, but it does so within the context of a vexing modern constraint too little noted. Zbigniew Brzezinski, responding to the observation that "the political structure of the state guarantees the relativism of all values through constitutional protections," noted how "the traditional socializing institutions—the family, the school, and the church [when] fully intact . . . provided a moral grounding, a counterbalance to the indulgent propaganda of the mass media" ("Weak Ramparts of the Permissive West," 56).

Significantly, regarding the fundamental doctrine of "moral agency" (D&C 101:78), the Lord conjoins individual accountability and constitutional freedoms:

"And that law of the land which is constitutional, supporting that *principle of freedom in maintaining rights and privileges, belongs to all mankind,* and is justifiable before me" (D&C 98:5; italics added).

Why is all this so vital?

"That every man may act in doctrine and principle pertaining to futurity, according to the moral agency which I have given unto him, that every man may be accountable for his own sins in the day of judgment" (D&C 101:78).

Sixty-two years after King Benjamin's warning, we read:

"For as their laws and their governments were established by the voice of the people, and they who chose evil were more numerous than they who chose good, therefore they were ripening for destruction, for the laws had become corrupted [30 B.C.]" (Helaman 5:2).

It has happened, and it may again.

Entitlement to the blessings of God ebbs and flows, and nadirs do occur.

"Now it is not common that the voice of the people desireth anything contrary to that which is right; but it is common for the lesser part of the people to desire that which is not right; therefore this shall ye observe and make it your law—to do your business by the voice of the people.

"And if the time comes that the voice of the people doth choose iniquity, then is the time that the judgments of God will come upon you; yea, then is the time he will visit you with great destruction even as he has hitherto visited this land" (Mosiah 29:26–27).

The "precepts of men" in decline can give ascendency to that which is more fashionable than it is constitutional (D&C 45:29).

A people, for instance, can actually lose the capacity for genuine self-governance by losing one of its precious prerequisites: "Obedience to the Unenforceable." Lord Moulton, the originator of that perceptive phrase, focused on an individual's obedience to that "which he cannot be forced to obey," which, significantly, Moulton, nearly eighty years ago, linked to "Free Choice" ("Law and Manners," 1).

For instance, would we approve the wickedness which characterized ancient Sodom and Gomorrah, if they balanced their budgets? It may be true, for instance, that the people of Sodom and Gomorrah had absolute free speech, but did they have anything worth saying? Those surfeited in sensualism may produce sounds, all right, but scarcely the informing, enlivening, and enriching speech which John Stuart Mill and our Founding Fathers had in mind.

CONVERSION

FACING, AS WE CLEARLY DO, the stark realities of trying to help those who are *uninvolved, unordained, untithed, unendowed,* and *unsealed*—in effect, the *unconverted*—we use the words *baptism, testimony,* and *conversion* carelessly, even interchangeably. Yet baptism is an *event,* whereas conversion is a *process.*

There can be baptism without testimony. There can be testimony without engaging in the process of becoming even as Jesus is (see 3 Nephi 27:27), but there cannot be conversion without testimony and without baptism by fire and water (see D&C 33:11).

Soberingly, Elder Marion G. Romney taught:

"Membership in the Church and conversion are not necessarily synonymous. Being converted, as we are here using the term, and having a testimony are not necessarily the same thing either. A testimony comes when the Holy Ghost gives the earnest seeker a witness of the truth. A moving testimony vitalizes faith; that is, it induces repentance and obedience to the commandments. Conversion, on the other hand, is the fruit of, or the reward for, repentance and obedience. (Of course one's testimony continues to increase as he is converted.)" (Conference Report, October 1963, 24).

Of true conversion, President Harold B. Lee said: "The greatest responsibility that a member of Christ's church has ever had is to become truly converted—and it is just as important to *stay* converted. . . .

" . . . One is converted when he sees with his eyes what he ought to see; when he hears with his ears what he ought to hear; and when he understands with his heart what he ought to understand—then he is converted" ("When Your Heart Tells You Things Your Mind Does Not Know," 3; italics in original).

Elder Bruce R. McConkie wrote several times of conversion, using Peter as an example. Peter, who had a testimony and who had witnessed miracles, nevertheless was instructed, "When thou art converted, strengthen thy brethren" (Luke 22:32). Yet, "after all the experience he had had, after all the testimonies he had borne, how is it [Peter] could not yet be classified as a convert? . . . There was something more that was going to come into the life of Peter to convert him, something more than already had come, in spite of all the marvelous things that he had seen and in which he had participated" (*Sermons and Writings*, 128).

"Conversion is to put off the natural man and to become a Saint by the power of the atoning sacrifice of Christ. . . . It does not happen and cannot happen unless and until someone gets the sanctifying power of the Holy Ghost into their lives" (McConkie, *Sermons and Writings*, 135).

"With most people, the conversion is a process; and it goes step by step, degree by degree, level by level, from a lower state to a higher, from grace to grace, until the time that the individual is wholly turned to the cause of righteousness . . . , until we become, literally, as the Book of Mormon says, Saints of God instead of natural men (Mosiah 3:19). What we are striving to do is to be converted" (McConkie, *Sermons and Writings,* 137).

If truly converted unto the Lord, we will really strive to be like Him (see 3 Nephi 27:27).

If we are not diverted from the word of God, which has a more powerful effect upon the minds of people than anything else, we will thereby hasten God's work (see Alma 31:5). Strange, nevertheless, that we should keep turning from that which brings the highest yield to lesser substitutes. There are so many ways in which we can "leave the word of God, and serve tables" (Acts 6:2).

In what is set forth regarding conversion, we find the repeated appearance of such words as *healing, seeing, word of God, feeling,* and *converted.* Jesus tells us we are to "continue to minister" to those who are disaffected, because we don't know who will come back or why or when. Jesus cautions, "I shall heal them" (3 Nephi 18:32). We shouldn't make the mistake of thinking that we, ourselves, can heal people. He heals them! He cauterizes our wounds with His healing power.

Still, He comforts us by saying we can "be the means of bringing salvation" to others (3 Nephi 18:32). We are working with a net that gathers of every kind (see Matthew 13:47).

A prophet inquired of yet another people, "If ye have felt to sing the song of redeeming love, . . . can ye *feel* so *now?*" (Alma 5:26; italics added). Those feelings of renewal are actuated by the Spirit, too.

We all exclaim over the verse in the Book of Mormon about those who were "converted unto the Lord, [and] never did fall away" (Alma 23:6). One can't help but envy that outcome, but we seldom pay attention to the prepositional phrase "converted *unto the Lord,*" the best adhesive to ensure our discipleship.

The Church's *General Handbook of Instructions* says: "Individuals have the primary responsibility for their own conversion." We can help others as we remember and nourish them "by the good word of God," but their agency finally prevails (Moroni 6:4).

The same *Handbook* also aptly observes, "Conversion is a lifelong process." No wonder we are in so many different stages in the conversion process! In a world in which there is a growing expectation of effortless entitlements, let us avoid having people feel the Church will take care of everything.

When Jesus commends individuals in the scriptures, He commends them for their traits or qualities of character, such as "unwearyingness" (Helaman 10:4–5) or, as with Hyrum Smith, "integrity" (D&C 124:15), for such "great faith" was "not found . . . in Israel" (Matthew 8:10).

President Gordon B. Hinckley rounds out the portrait of a performing disciple:

"When there throbs in the heart of an individual Latter-day Saint a great and vital testimony of the truth of this work, he will be found doing his duty in the Church. He will be found in his sacrament meetings. He will be found in his priesthood meetings. He will be found paying his honest tithes and offerings. He will be doing his home teaching. He will be found in attendance at the temple as frequently as his circumstances will permit. He will have within him a great desire to share the gospel with others. He will be found strengthening and lifting his brethren and sisters. It is conversion that makes the difference" (cited in "News of the Church," 99).

The commendations of the Lord concern these very basic, central virtues which we must mirror even more. What we are dealing with is clearly a process. Sometimes it has barely started in new members and often it is not ever really pursued. Hence the churn in the Church which doesn't solely involve new converts we fail to retain—but also the in-and-out of some old-timers. The churn will go on in the absence of real conversion. Confirmingly, Peter and Paul write about our need to become "rooted," "grounded," "stablished," and "settled" (Colossians 2:7; 1:23; Ephesians 3:17).

The process is for all with no exemptions. The Lord said to the modern Twelve:

"And after their temptations, and much tribulation, behold, I, the Lord, will *feel* after them, and if they harden not their hearts, and stiffen not their necks against me, they shall be *converted,* and I will *heal* them" (D&C 112:13; italics added).

We compound the challenge by assuming that telling is teaching. If a one-way telling worked all by itself, we'd be overtaking the City of Enoch by now!

Therefore, we can be magnified in our callings in proportion to how we magnify Jesus and draw closer to Him. We, too, can *"feel* and *see"* (3 Nephi 18:25; italics added). After all, Jesus "was wounded for our transgressions, he was bruised for our iniquities; . . . and with his stripes we are *healed"* (Mosiah 14:5; italics added).

As Elder Marion G. Romney observed, an individual so converted "would walk in *newness of life"* (see Romans 6:4); he *feels* he has *"joy"* and *"peace of conscience"* (Mosiah 4:3; italics added). In this quiet but powerful and penetrating process of conversion, said Elder Romney, the individual "will recognize it by the way he *feels*" (Conference Report, October 1963, 23, 25; italics added).

How can we know how we are doing? Jesus says, in effect, we are heaven-bound if we are becoming more childlike (see Matthew 18:3). King Benjamin delineated that kind of childlikeness: "Submissive, meek, humble, patient, full of love, willing to submit to all things which the Lord seeth fit to inflict upon him, even as a child doth submit to his father" (Mosiah 3:19).

Another measure is the degree to which we are giving "away all [our] sins" in order to know God better (Alma 22:18). All real disciples believe in and apply the Atonement regularly in their lives, shedding sins and shortcomings along the way.

WHAT MANNER OF MEN OUGHT WE TO BE?

ANCIENTLY, THE RESURRECTED Savior asked of priesthood leaders, searchingly: "What manner of men ought ye to be?" (3 Nephi 27:27). Jesus then prescribed that we should be even as He is.

We should be striving, attribute by attribute, to become more and more like Him, including by developing the spiritual manners that accompany living "after the manner of happiness" (2 Nephi 5:27).

Putting off "the natural man" and becoming, instead, a "man of Christ" does not usually occur quickly, but rather "in process of time" (Mosiah 3:19; Helaman 3:29; Moses 7:21).

Whether quietly exemplifying for our families or for our Church flocks, there is no substitute for this eloquence of example with its lastingness and contagiousness.

JOSEPH SMITH

The Prophet declared: "I never told you I was perfect; but there is no error in the revelations which I have taught" (Smith, *Discourses of the Prophet Joseph Smith,* 66; or *History of the Church,* 6:366).

This is my bedrock testimony, too!

Furthermore, the revelations Joseph taught to us are so remarkable, they could have come from only One Source.

For his imperfections and shortcomings, the Prophet Joseph was accountable, as are we. Our loving Lord will help all who will work through their imperfections, be they large or small. Meanwhile, we can draw upon the cascade of revelations that rains upon us through the remarkable Prophet Joseph Smith!

FAITH EVEN WHEN . . .

President Marion G. Romney, upon entering the First Presidency, said in his ward sacrament meeting:

"I have always sustained the President of the Church, and I can sustain him now, even when he calls me as a counselor."

As usual, there was wisdom in his wit.

PRIESTHOOD

We are to focus on helping others, yet there are some things *only others* can do for themselves. Thus, *authority* in the priesthood is given through ordination, but *power* in the priesthood is received through righteous living.

None of us can merely sit back and wait for the power to develop. Both the power and the authority of example remain for us to develop.

DAILY, NOT PERIODIC, DISCIPLESHIP

IN HIGHER EDUCATION WE SPEAK often of student credit hours. Analogously, the plan of salvation produces what might be called "disciple credit hours." Furthermore, we are not merely auditing life's courses but, instead, taking life's "classes" for credit, thereby accumulating character—the lasting coin of the Regal Realm.

These ongoing spiritual "courses" include the equivalents of general education—the trials, temptations, and afflictions which are, said Paul, "common to man" (1 Corinthians 10:13)—along with upper-division work, and then very customized curricula for the meek and the righteous: postdoctoral work. In sum, these experiences constitute daily discipleship.

Furthermore, our enrollment in these individual-ized "classes" may not be highly visible to others, and even our own awareness of this on-going, precious process is often minimal. Hence, such courses are embedded in every life situation to some degree. *What we are* and *what we are becoming* are, therefore, what matters, even if some do not acknowledge that they are thus enrolled!

President Brigham Young said with painful clarity of life's daily micromoments:

"It is the aggregate of the acts which I perform through life that makes up the conduct that will be exhibited in the day of judgment, and when the books are opened, there will be the life which I have lived for me to look upon, and there also will be the acts of your lives for you to look upon. Do you not know that the building up of the kingdom of God . . . is to be done by little acts? You breathe one breath at a time; each moment is set apart to its act, and each act to its moment. It is the moments and the little acts that make the sum of the life of man. Let every second, minute, hour, and day we live be spent in doing that which we know to be right" (*Journal of Discourses*, 3:342–43).

In all these "little acts," as President Young called them, do we worship Jesus enough to strive to be like Him? (see 3 Nephi 27:27). This is the comprehensive exam! Many things that are hard to measure now ultimately matter most.

Postdoctoral credit is a highly individualized thing. Remarkable Moses had been wearied because the children of Israel were restless. They were thirsty, unremembering, and ungrateful. In a place called Meribah, Moses—one of the greatest souls ever—was stressed, wearied, burned out, or whatever they called "people fatigue" in those days. The scriptures say that momentarily frustrated, Moses "spake unadvisedly," saying, "Must *we* fetch you water?" (Psalm 106:33; Numbers 20:10; italics added).

He had a little pronoun problem, and yet the Lord mentored him and tutored him and brought him along, so that Moses would not be confused about who had brought forth the water from the rock. It is a high compliment for the Lord to mentor and tutor us, and Moses handled that mentoring well.

A wintry verse of scripture reads, "He trieth their patience and their faith" (Mosiah 23:21). If we do not understand this fact, we will misread life. But why does God try our faith and patience in particular? Why not try our ability to make money or to amass political power? The Lord is not concerned with these skills. Patience, however, is an eternal quality. It is portable. So is faith. These qualities are out of the developmental reach of those who are caught up in the cares of the world.

The straight and narrow path is well posted with warnings of such common failures as misusing authority, covering our sins, and gratifying our vain ambitions. These negative traits can be seen in a bookkeeper as well as in a dishonest CEO. Such falsifying can be displayed by a prominent political leader or by a plumber.

Because we are all imperfect, much generosity is called for. Sir Thomas More had just been condemned by his ungenerous jury, and then More, in one of those acts of public magnanimity, said, "I verily trust and shall therefore right heartily pray, that though your lordships have now here in earth been judges to my condemnation, we may yet hereafter in heaven merrily all meet together, to our everlasting salvation" (cited in Kenny, *Thomas More*, 88).

Sir Thomas More, along with many others, gives us a benchmark of courage to consider, though he was not generous with heroic Tyndale! David Daniell observed of More: "It remains curious, to put it mildly, that the gravitational pull of Sir Thomas More has been allowed to distort Tyndale's orbit, especially as More's dealings with Tyndale were coloured by near-rabid hatred. More had fine qualities, but they did not show when he attacked the reformers" (*William Tyndale*, 4).

Magnanimity, however, doesn't have to occur in front of an assemblage of lords—it can occur privately, as in a marriage when someone displays graciousness and magnanimity.

Where are the classrooms in this process of spiritual education? They are in friendships, at school or university, in family life, in civic clubs, in politics—all offering opportunities for the taming of ourselves and our egos.

And the teacher is often the Holy Ghost.

THE HOLY GHOST AND REVELATION

IN THE VERY BEGINNING, after Eden, witnessing revelation was needed by Adam: "And in that day the Holy Ghost fell upon Adam, which beareth record of the Father and the Son" (Moses 5:9). This is still the principal mission of the Holy Ghost, "which witnesses of the Father and the Son" and glorifies Christ (2 Nephi 31:18; see also John 16:14).

Therefore, it is our duty and privilege, as Church members, to receive personal revelation from the Holy Ghost, confirming that "Jesus Christ is the Son of God, and that he was crucified for the sins of the world" (D&C 46:13). If we are built upon the Rock of our

Redeemer, the promise is that we will not be dragged down amid life's storms (see Helaman 5:12). The metaphor is apt, embodying as it does the relentlessness of the daily tugs and downward pulls of the world.

Having the witness about our Savior is vital for us not only personally but as shepherds of families and Church flocks. Among our Church flocks are some to whom "it is given to believe on [our] words, that they also might have eternal life if they continue faithful" (D&C 46:14). Hence, we need to know for their sakes, too.

OBTAINING REVELATION

Enos's struggling reminds us of Oliver Cowdery's struggle to obtain revelation. It requires serious, mental effort on our part—taking real thought, not just asking perfunctorily—and also faithfully continuing as we commenced (see D&C 9:7).

Revelation is a matter not of pushing buttons but of pushing ourselves, aided by fasting, scripture study, and personal pondering. On occasion, revelation may come to the righteous unsolicited.

Revelation requires us to have a sufficient degree of personal righteousness to be admitted regularly to the process.

The Holy Ghost cannot be stopped at national borders, and revelation requires no visa!

STRETCHING THE SINEWS OF THE MIND

At times, we can speak words well beyond our own capacity. As President Marion G. Romney observed, "I always know when I am speaking under the inspiration of the Holy Ghost because I always learn something from what I've said" (cited in Packer, *Teach Ye Diligently,* 357).

Experience with revelation naturally has its beginnings and then builds on itself, just as the Prophet Joseph taught:

"A person may profit by noticing the first intimation of the spirit of revelation; for instance, when you feel pure intelligence flowing into you, it may give you sudden strokes of ideas" (*Teachings of the Prophet Joseph Smith,* 151).

Since there are other enticing voices in the world, remember that God entices us to do good, to love Him, and to serve Him. God safeguards this sacred process, so that with increasing experience, we "may know with a perfect knowledge, as the daylight is from the dark night" (Moroni 7:15).

But the scriptures assure us that God's words come "not only [to] men but women also. Now this is not all; little children do have words given unto them many times, which confound the wise and the learned" (Alma 32:23).

Likewise, the Spirit serves by bringing us much needed personal peace and consolation, especially in a world full of "perplexities," "commotion," and "wars and rumors of wars" (D&C 88:79, 91; 45:26). After all, the Comforter is a comforter who helps us, among other things, to avoid growing weary and fainting in our minds (see Hebrews 12:3).

Very importantly, when the nations of the earth are

in distress "with perplexity" (Luke 21:25), we can receive spiritual confirmation that the directions being given by Church leaders truly are given to "guide us in these latter days" ("We Thank Thee, O God, for a Prophet," *Hymns,* no. 19; see also D&C 42:61).

DIRECTIONS WITHOUT EXPLANATIONS

We sometimes receive divine directions without detailed explanations. Sometimes, too, after taking much thought and studying things, revelation consists of connecting previously incomplete insights; of an instant, things are crystal clear and "fitly framed together" (Ephesians 2:21).

Very importantly, the Holy Ghost brings needed things to our remembrance, so we should prepare by "treasuring up" precious things in our individual storehouses of memory. All of this can come "into [our] hearts, . . . in the very hour, yea, in the very moment" (D&C 100:5–6).

Revelation follows proper channels, of course. Lay members do not receive doctrinal revelation for the whole Church, which is the role of the president and prophet of the Church.

Directional revelation is given for the whole Church by the Lord's prophet. Such directional revelation occurred when President Lorenzo Snow was moved upon to emphasize the need for more Church members to pay a full tithing. Likewise, President Gordon B. Hinckley was clearly inspired to direct the surge in the building of so many temples so that more faithful members—worldwide—could receive their temple blessings. It was not only what the Lord wanted done but it was also according to the Lord's timing.

EXPLANATIONS, TOO!

Scriptures beget even more scriptures. The Prophet Joseph Smith was spiritually stirred while reading a scripture from John (see John 5:29). He then received the expansive, instructive, and precious revelation now known as Doctrine and Covenants 76.

When President Joseph F. Smith had been reading

and pondering verses in Peter, he received the striking and illuminating Doctrine and Covenants 138, concerning the work in the spirit world.

THE MIND AND HEART

Most revelation comes in the following manner: "I will tell you *in your mind* and *in your heart, by the Holy Ghost*" (D&C 8:2; italics added). For instance, as we "liken" certain scriptures to ourselves, we must remember both intellect and feeling are involved (1 Nephi 19:23).

When Enos was "struggling in the spirit, . . . the voice of the Lord came into [his] mind again" (Enos 1:10). The voice of the Spirit need not pass through eardrums; instead, the words go directly to our minds—audibly and distinctly.

Feelings without words can come, too, giving needed directions. Whether by words or by feelings, there will also be an accompanying sense of peace. This confirming peacefulness is such a reassuring blessing!

DEFLECTING THE DEFINING MOMENTS

There are moments when people are touched by the Spirit, but they try to rationalize. They try to finesse what could be a defining moment, as King Agrippa did. Paul bore a powerful testimony to Agrippa. Yet, it would have been politically incorrect for him to be identified with Paul. Wily Agrippa dodgingly responded, "Almost thou persuadest me to be a Christian" (Acts 26:28).

ONE PING ONLY

In *The Hunt for Red October,* the defecting Soviet sea captain had to send a signal of intent to the American sub which would not be misunderstood. The sea captain instructed his radar man to send the signal—but *"one ping only."* The situation was so delicate, even the slightest mistake could cost lives and start a war.

The Holy Ghost can elect to communicate with precision and brevity—"one ping only"—lest in the mortal cacophony we do not hear simple, divine instructions.

GENUINE TWO-WAY COMMUNICATION

The Holy Ghost brings about genuine, two-way communication—something unfortunately rare in many human communications. The scriptures reassuringly declare: "When a man speaketh by the power of the Holy Ghost the power of the Holy Ghost carrieth it unto the hearts of the children of men" and "he that receiveth the word by the Spirit of truth receiveth it as it is preached by the Spirit of truth" (2 Nephi 33:1; D&C 50:21).

This two-way communication occurs during inspired teaching in a classroom, while speaking in sacrament meeting, or during quiet conversations one with another.

HOW VITAL IS THE HOLY GHOST?

Any one of the following reasons, by itself, shows

how absolutely vital the Holy Ghost is, and in the aggregate they are overwhelming!

1. Without Him and the baptism by fire, we cannot be saved (see John 3:5).

2. Only by Him and through Him can we really know and truly testify that Jesus is the Christ (see D&C 20:26–27).

3. He quickens "the inner man," helping us to put off the natural man in order to become truly converted (Ephesians 3:16; Moses 6:65).

4. He even gives power to angels to speak—and can do likewise with us (see 2 Nephi 32:3).

5. *He knows all things!* (see Moroni 10:5; D&C 35:19).

Clearly, He is not merely a line on an organizational chart or part of a procedural checklist. Nor is He someone with whom we can be content to have merely a nodding acquaintance, or consider an object of periodic contemplation, or reduce to a bumper-sticker.

He is actually involved with all that really matters. If we cultivate this Gift, we access the powers of the universe. No wonder we are to "stir up" and "quench not" that great gift (2 Timothy 1:6; 1 Thessalonians 5:19).

He can be our constant Companion! (see D&C 121:46).

REFLECTIONS ON GOSPEL TRUTHS AND PRINCIPLES

ADVERSITY

As life's events bring our allotment of adversity, let us accept the bitter cup without becoming bitter. By so doing, we will testify in special and contagious ways!

A friend who lost his second wife to cancer heard a well-meaning friend say, "Why should you have to go through this again?" Full of quiet faith, he replied, "Why not?"

FATHER'S BLESSING

My father's blessing came later in my life. Even so, it anticipated my major illness by twenty years. My meek father blessed me with the "strength to bear the burdens which may come upon you in physical ways . . . that you may bear [them] as [Paul] did, without complaint."

I continue to strive to come closer to that stretching goal.

PREPARING FOR LIVING IN A CELESTIAL CULTURE

We become so locked into the cadence of the cares of the world.

Because we should be preparing to live forever in a celestial culture, whatever exists contrarily in our temporary, local cultures must finally fall by the way—like so much old scaffolding. Besides, the fleeting fashions of the world will pass, ere long, and become obsolete anyway (see 1 Corinthians 7:31).

We do not need to store a year's supply of obsolescence!

MUSIC IN HELL

Brigham Young said, "There is no music in hell" (*Journal of Discourses,* 9:244). However, some loud sounds are currently masquerading as music—which would seem to help qualify hell as hell.

BEING IN BONDAGE

Earlier in life, one trades time for money; later, money for time. Some unfortunates have too little of either to negotiate.

Peter stated that bondage involves more than physical slavery: "Of whom a man is overcome, of the same is he brought in bondage" (2 Peter 2:19). Embedded in the Doctrine and Covenants is the piercing declaration: "It is not right that any man should be in bondage one to another" (D&C 101:79).

Do we, therefore, really seek to assess the various forms of bondage that we have allowed to afflict us? These chains may not be visible, but they are there and are experienced, such as chronic grumpiness and untamed egos, etc. Drugs and pornography now enslave millions more than were physically enslaved in the American South before and during the Civil War.[1] It is very difficult to leave the bondage of these "plantations."

NEEDLESS DISTRACTIONS

In the same way that a whiff of bad breath can detract from a whispered compliment, a lack of meekness can likewise diminish the impact of one's testimony.

FILTERS

The filter of selfishness is like trying to hear a supernal symphony through defective hearing aids. Single notes get through but not the harmony.

MEEKNESS

Dozens of biographies have underscored, for me, the crucial role of the meekness and greatness of soul.

Significant contributions are made by the unmeek, to be sure, and unanchored genius can still bless mankind. Nevertheless, the master spirits, the truly great ones, always display a goodly measure of meekness!

THE ONSLAUGHT

In the here and now, God permits an obvious

onslaught of evil, so gross it staggers us at times. It will get worse. We suffer mostly because of the abuse of agency "here and now" by us and others. Yet agency is the price of eternal joy "there and then."

Though God permits, that does not mean He causes or endorses the misuse of mortals' freedom to choose:

"Many things occur in the world in which it seems very difficult for most of us to find a solid reason for the acknowledgment of the hand of the Lord. I have come to the belief that the only reason I have been able to discover by which we should acknowledge the hand of God in some occurrences is the fact that the thing which has occurred has been permitted of the Lord" (Smith, "Message to the Soldier Boys of 'Mormondom,'" 821).

While we noddingly assent to these revealed words, we seldom stretch our minds to explore their implications.

PERSONAL SUFFERING

Those who do not repent must suffer even as Jesus did, though not on the same, immense scale as in the awful arithmetic of His atonement. Nevertheless, they must experience before the resurrection real misery and pay a real, personal price (see Alma 40:15). There is no free pass, and a mere "few stripes" will not suffice (2 Nephi 28:8).

A SIGH OF ACCOMPLISHMENT

There are times when we need not be embarrassed to sing, "I have *fought* my way through" ("Come, Let Us Anew," *Hymns,* no. 217; italics added).

WAITING

We must wait until an errant individual is willing to receive the Holy Ghost. We cannot force that moment. Given their agency, individuals must desire to be touched by Him. Thus, we are to "continue to minister" until a person desires change; he, alone, can decide to engage with the Holy Spirit (3 Nephi 18:32). Thus we cannot force things, but we can "continue to minister."

Yes, we go on trying, even when our witness is unheeded. The Lord has told us firmly how this process works (see D&C 68:3–5). After all, God is in the business of saving souls. It is His work and glory (see Moses 1:39). We must consider the wait as part of life and part of His work. Ironically, while we are to "wait upon the Lord" (2 Nephi 18:17), He must also wait for us.

ON NOT QUITTING

We must not quit trying. If we do, then the natural man has won another battle, and we are, in effect, acknowledging that the doctrine of hope does not amount to much. Periodic exhorters are like a spent roman candle that puffs and flares for a brief moment and then, mute and charred, expires.

Refraining from giving up on others is, therefore, a special form of giving. Otherwise, hope is sidelined and loses its rightful place, which is "smiling brightly before

us" ("We Thank Thee, O God, for a Prophet," *Hymns,*
no. 19).

SCAR TISSUE

There are two reasons to look beyond the scar tissue
of the past. One is empathy. The other is that such tissue merely represents *what once was,* not *what is becoming,* as to present spiritual muscles. Proud flesh—the
extinct remains of the past—is appropriately named.

A SHOEHORN

Obedience can be like a helpful shoehorn, easing us
wincingly into new and spiritual symmetry, as our
swollen pride gives way.

MEMORIES

Some memories are exclusive and personal. Others
are shared. The former, however, are especially able to
move us, to brace us, and to caress us. The quiet massage
of memories brings personal refreshment and renewal.

DEEP THINGS

As with the doctrine of spiritual submissiveness and agency, we may come late in life to an appreciation of the "deep things" of God (1 Corinthians 2:10).

Deep, yes, but not because they are abstract or complex. Ironically, their mysteriousness lies in their simpleness. They are "plain," and we are surprised upon finally discovering their obviousness that their deepness actually reflects their pervasiveness.

Like ever-present gravity, deep things are so obvious as to go unreflected upon; nevertheless, there are constant consequences. We have been looking "beyond the mark" (Jacob 4:14) all the time, deliberately and strangely seeking instead for things we could not understand.

WHICH TEARS?

Seeing with even a modicum of empathy the various and wrenching sufferings of others, we cannot refrain from weeping for each one. But which floodgate should we open first?

BLESSINGS

When we forget God and His blessings, we first cease counting them and, finally, we do not remember them at all. Unnumbered, they soon slip the bonds of consciousness.

That can even occur on a larger, dramatic scale: "People began to forget those signs and wonders which they had heard, and began to be less and less astonished . . . and began to disbelieve all which they had heard and seen" (3 Nephi 2:1).

Being dragged down can expunge even the astonishing!

HONEST RELATIVISM

If, as some say, there are no moral absolutes, why do some *rage* against good things? Why not merely express a little *relative* indignation and let it go at that?

Rapid Decay

When some individuals fray and unravel, it seems to happen so fast. They have no brakes, and they crash through one restraining barricade after another, leaving no skid marks. Onlookers are surprised at the ghastly momentum this process acquires—undoubtedly propelled by pride. All the while such individuals feed on wafer-thin rationalizations.

Twisted Tolerance

We need to sharpen the distinction between loving and worshiping God with all of our heart, mind, and soul, and loving our neighbor, for we are to love and worship God but are not to worship our neighbor (see D&C 59:5–6).

The first commandment is, after all, the *first* commandment (see Matthew 22:38–40).

Many do well at keeping both the first and second great commandments. Many profess belief but neglect their neighbors. Some, however, ironically focus on the second commandment to the diminution of the first.

Others are free to choose, of course, but shoulder-shrugging indifference and indulgence toward others scarcely qualify as loving one's neighbor. Live and let die is thus a strange application of tolerance.

The Countenance

When spiritual decay occurs, it is almost as if a physical light goes out in the countenance of such individuals. It is surely not Jesus whose image they have in their countenance (see Alma 5:14).

Opaqueness, instead of radiance, sets in. Sometimes not a flicker of light is to be seen!

No Exemptions

Those who are high achievers and highly devoted to their secular specialty—but often to the exclusion of God—nevertheless display a commendable and beneficial discipline in that thing, bringing them success and blessing others. Their egos can facilitate unusual achievement, but the challenge of bypassing spiritual submissiveness must be paid.

It happens if our hobbies and specialties become obsessions performed to the exclusion of worship of God. Then there is no way—however well we keep the other commandments—that we can truly keep the first commandment: worshiping Him with all our hearts and minds. Nevertheless, though the contribution made by such sincere individuals may still benefit many, it keeps such individuals from coming off conqueror in the real contest of life (see D&C 10:5).

Hence, the mortal prizes of today are often deserved, but those who win them "have their reward" (Matthew 6:2). Such prizes are not timeless. Some are beckoned by the mirage that is the praise of man. Others feel a certain security, though false, when ensconced behind their Maginot lines of expertise.

How important now, and where now, are the synagogues in which some so desperately craved a place that they would not declare for Jesus?

How important is a line in a resume if it comes at the expense and neglect of loved ones?

NOTE

1. "According to the National Household Survey on Drug Abuse (NHSDA), there were 14.8 million illicit drug users aged 12 and older in the United States in 1999" ("Drug Threats—Marijuana," 7). "The slave population actually grew from less than a million in 1787 to an estimated four million by the early 1860's" (Eason, "Hallelujah—Juneteenth Is Here!" 2).

BLESSED RENEWALS

THE PROMISE IS FAMILIAR THAT the Lord will renew us in body—no small thing for those who seek to serve Him with "unwearyingness" (Helaman 10:4–5; see also D&C 84:33). During these blessed renewals, there will be times when the Spirit will wash over us like surf—to refresh us, to reassure us, and sometimes to brace us.

The Holy Ghost will let us know unmistakably that the overseeing Lord of the Universe knows and loves us—personally! "His hand [is] in all things" (D&C 59:21), for He is in the details of our lives so far as our agency allows. He is mindful of His people in every nation (see Alma 26:37).

THE SPIRIT WORLD AND PARADISE

The conditions in paradise are described by Alma as "a state of happiness," "a state of rest," "a state of peace," a state of "rest from all [our] troubles and from all care, and sorrow" (Alma 40:12). We can scarcely imagine those emancipatory conditions. Given such descriptions, paradise will be paradise, and the righteous will be no strangers there.

Rest from the troubles, cares, and sorrows of the world, by itself, will be an enormous event. Whether this occurs because we gain added perspective, with our worries falling like so much scaffolding, or from a combination of things, we do not know now.

Meanwhile, the wicked are in a "state of misery" before the resurrection (Alma 40:15). Though we do not have details, President Joseph F. Smith's vision (D&C 138) informs us that the righteous in the spirit world preach the gospel to those in the spirit prison. Can some, if they accept the gospel in spirit prison and under certain guidelines, be emancipated to enter paradise *before* the resurrection?

Being freed from the pressing cares of the world means just that. Beset as we are now, we cannot imagine such an anticipation. Nagging worry-lists so dominate daily life.

President Charles W. Penrose said: "The knowledge of our former state has fled from us. . . . The veil is drawn between us and our former habitation. This is for our trial. If we could see the things of eternity, and comprehend ourselves as we are; if we could penetrate the mists and clouds that shut out eternal realities from our gaze, the fleeting things of time would be no trial to us, and one of the great objects of our earthly probation or testing would be lost. But the past has gone from our memory, the future is shut out from our vision and we are living here in time, to learn little by little, line upon line, precept upon precept. Here in the darkness, in the sorrow, in the trial, in the pain, in the adversity, we have to learn what is right and distinguish it from what is wrong, and lay hold of right and truth and learn to live it" (*Journal of Discourses*, 26:28).

If God blocks out the memory of our first estate while we are here in the second estate, to make choosing fair and just and a matter of faith, does He also block off the memory of the second estate when we go to the spirit world?

Perhaps the memories of the mortal second estate are had by all in the spirit world, thus giving those who are disbelievers here some advantage there. Perhaps the memories of the second estate are accessed only by those in paradise. In any case, those in the spirit world must accept and have faith in the gospel and receive the Holy Ghost, if they are to move from the spirit prison to paradise. If not, why send the missionaries to the spirit world?

Spirit prison is a term that may seem too harsh, too graphic, and too simplistic. Yet it describes unmistakably a restraining barrier that actually exists. Only further revelation will supply details.

ON DYING

I go on the remainder of my journey, short as it may be, through the process of dying, with a calmness and with these reflections.

Though a severe limitation, fatigue can be an accompanying friend in the process of dying.

Some anxieties are understandably common to life's exit routes leading to death. Later, when we look back after the trip through the veil, our anxieties will turn out to be naive and perhaps even amusing. After all, in gospel grammar, death is not an exclamation point, merely a comma. Nevertheless, dying is a new, individual experience.

> *For those paradise-bound,*
> *What seemed to be the grim ballet of separation,*
> *With but one pirouette,*
> *Turns out to be a resplendent reunion.*

My Testimony

My testimony covers the range of all that I have learned through the Spirit, through the scriptures, through life, and through the mentoring of others. Because God's is an inexhaustible gospel, it keeps growing, including Heavenly Father's stretching plan of salvation, which is clearly the best way for His dealings with the human family to achieve our eventual happiness, justice, and joy.

I exclaim of our Creator's cosmos. It is overwhelming, it is stunning, and it accords completely with Heavenly Father's plans for each one of us.

I testify, too, that His hand is there in ways we

scarcely appreciate—as in the preparation for the framing and ratifying and implementing of the United States Constitution, in which we see His majesty—as well as in those cosmic things of the universe.

I gladly testify of the remarkable manner in which the Restoration occurred and marvel at how the Lord, using imperfect people, can proceed with His perfect work. And in particular, I look to the day when mankind will yet proclaim the Book of Mormon from the housetops, providing a more distinct alternative to human indifference, despair, and yearning.

I witness with equal strength to the handing down of the keys of the Holy Apostleship held by Joseph Smith and currently by President Gordon B. Hinckley, as they will be held by subsequent Church presidents.

It has always been easy for me to believe in God. I have struggled with my own impatience at times but not the basic doctrines. Everything attests to God's goodness and His majesty—whether it is the universe He has created or us as His spirit sons and daughters, or the raising up of a nation centered on the need to have moral agency. Every sign and indicator, as well as the whisperings of the Spirit, converge gracefully in my testimony of this great latter-day work.

Therefore, I thank and worship Heavenly Father for all that He has done in His plan by insisting on our agency in order that we might have joy. So also I thank and worship Jesus for all that He has done through the marvelous and great atonement, as things come to pass in the Lord's due time.

I believe there is a "time appointed for every man" (D&C 121:25). When that time comes, one is enveloped, as it becomes "Passengers only beyond this point."

There is nothing like this work in all the world or in all of history, to which I gladly attest in growing gratitude and spiritual submissiveness which I share with my readers. Through it all, I have had a special wife, special parents, and special children and grandchildren to help me along the way.

It is truly a marvelous work and a wonder.

SOURCES

Anselm. *St. Anselm: Basic Writings.* Translated by Sidney Norton Deane. 2d ed. La Salle, Ill.: Open Court Publishing, 1948.

Bagehot, Walter. *The Works of Walter Bagehot.* Edited by Forrest Morgan. 5 vols. Hartford, Conn.: Travelers Insurance Company, 1891.

Brzezinski, Zbigniew. "Weak Ramparts of the Permissive West." In *At Century's End: Great Minds Reflect on Our Times.* Edited by Nathan P. Gardels. La Jolla, Calif.: ALTI Publishing, 1995.

Chernow, Ron. *Alexander Hamilton.* New York: Penguin Press, 2004.

Clark, J. Reuben, Jr. *Behold the Lamb of God.* Salt Lake City: Deseret Book, 1991.

———. Conference Report, October 1953, 84.

Clark, Ronald W. *Einstein: The Life and Times.* New York: Avon Books, Discus Book, 1971.

Daniell, David. *William Tyndale: A Biography.* New Haven: Yale University Press, 2004.

Dyson, Freeman J. "Energy in the Universe." *Scientific American* 225, no. 3 (September 1971): 59.

Eason, Oscar, Jr. "Hallelujah—Juneteenth Is Here!" *Seattle Medium,* 19 June 2002.

Flexner, James Thomas. *Washington: The Indispensable Man.* Boston: Little, Brown, 1974.

Fischer, David Hackett. *Paul Revere's Ride.* New York: Oxford University Press, 1994.

General Handbook of Instructions. Salt Lake City: The Church of Jesus Christ of Latter-day Saints, 1998.

Heinrichs, Allison M. "The Stellar Census: 70 Sextillion." *Los Angeles Times,* 26 July 2003.

Hinckley, Gordon B. In "News of the Church." *Ensign,* May 1984, 99.

Holland, Matthew S. "'To Close the Circle of Our Felicities': *Caritas* and Jefferson's First Inaugural." *Review of Politics* 66, no. 2 (Spring 2004): 202.

Hymns of The Church of Jesus Christ of Latter-day Saints. Salt Lake City: The Church of Jesus Christ of Latter-day Saints, 1985.

Journal of Discourses. 26 vols. London: Latter-day Saints' Book Depot, 1854–86.

Kenny, Anthony. *Thomas More.* Oxford: Oxford University Press, 1983.

Lee, Harold B. "When Your Heart Tells You Things Your Mind Does Not Know." *New Era,* February 1971, 3.

Lewis, C. S. *The World's Last Night and Other Essays.* New York: Harcourt Brace Jovanovich, Harvest Books, 1973. Page 1101.

McConkie, Bruce R. *Sermons and Writings of Bruce R. McConkie.*

Edited by Mark L. McConkie. Salt Lake City: Bookcraft, 1998.

Moulton, Lord. "Law and Manners." *Atlantic Monthly* 134, no. 1 (July 1924): 1.

National Drug Intelligence Center. "Drug Threats—Marijuana." *United States–Canada Border Drug Threat Assessment,* December 2001.

Packer, Boyd K. *Teach Ye Diligently.* Revised edition. Salt Lake City: Deseret Book, 1991.

Romney, Marion G. Conference Report, October 1963, 23–25.

Sagan, Carl. *Cosmos.* New York: Random House, 1980.

Sandage, Allen. "A Scientist Reflects on Religious Belief." *Truth Journal* 1 (1985).

Smith, Jean Edward. *John Marshall: Definer of a Nation.* New York: Henry Holt, 1996.

Smith, Joseph. *Discourses of the Prophet Joseph Smith.* Compiled by Alma P. Burton. Salt Lake City: Deseret Book, 1977.

———. *History of The Church of Jesus Christ of Latter-day Saints.* Edited by B. H. Roberts. 2d ed. rev. 7 vols. Salt Lake City: The Church of Jesus Christ of Latter-day Saints, 1932–51.

———. *Teachings of the Prophet Joseph Smith.* Selected by Joseph Fielding Smith. Salt Lake City: Deseret Book, 1976.

Smith, Joseph F. *Gospel Doctrine.* 5th ed. Salt Lake City: Deseret Book, 1939.

———. "A Message to the Soldier Boys of 'Mormondom.'" *Improvement Era* 20, no. 9 (July 1917): 821.

Strauss, Stephen. "Clusters of Galaxies Form Pattern like

Honeycomb, Astronomy Teams Find." *Globe and Mail,* 5 February 1990.

Tuchman, Barbara W. *The March of Folly: From Troy to Vietnam.* New York: Alfred A. Knopf, 1984.

West, Morris L. *The Tower of Babel.* New York: William Morrow, 1968.

Woodruff, Wilford. Conference Report, April 1898, 89.

INDEX